BREATHING UNDERWATER

LISA DAVIDSON AND RALPH PETTY

Breathing Underwater

SYLPH EDITIONS

CONTENTS

For Alexia and Nico

Breathing underwater

THE FIRST GLINT of this collaboration appeared
at dinner, as we leaned in to toast a new project,
a challenge really, to see what would arise if we
overlapped our images and words. The idea was
to spark a dialogue that excluded description and
definition, direction and directive. Over the months,
a kind of underground railway was set up: drawings
appeared on a desk, poems settled in alongside them,
and we rarely, if ever, discussed process. Yet it set up a
quiet buzz of energy; maybe call it recognition.

This at first random collection became an unfolding
of ideas, a reflection of our inevitable and multiple
layers of collaboration, of our lives at that given
moment. Then we lost one of our own, and the story
began to acquire a specific arc: an exploration of the
underlying forces shifting the weave between us.

The mountains behind the house, the Tanargue,
are named for an ancient god of thunder. Storm clouds
gather there in heaps like sky-high tumbleweed,
trapped by the flanks of the hillsides. Lightning strikes
so often that the land is strewn with multiple old trees
burnt to the core. Ruthless and incalculable rifts,
overgrown with moss and bridged by new growth.
And that's where we finally landed, in a place where
the images speak for the words, the words paint
the pictures.

I Spectrum of Time

If blood pumped in sync with sap,
as slow as the seasons,
we could watch that tree grow.

Branches snaking out in a blur of speed,
capturing distracted lovers with
tendrils of spring growth.

One heartbeat a year and
we could watch mountains move.

Like the giant who lives underground
behind the house,
his stone knuckles pushing up,
just about to break the surface.

2 Polished stones

In a dream, of course, the choice arose:
fall back against the pillows, stasis, or follow option two –
somehow we got snagged together last night and the choice
was the familiar side of the bed
or the stranger next to me.

Stasis, fall back against the pillow,
or else slip through the cracks
to tomorrow, a foreign place.

Like polished stones tumbling for aeons down a river,
we bumped into each other
deep underwater.

I've rolled through the night with you,
you've skidded behind, but come daytime,
the light always gleams off the
shards of granite still rough.

3   Washed ashore

The spooky walk
starts before leaving home,
with ghosts tossed up on the stones
from the fog below.

Outside, it's all
hoots and pecks and barks and whoops,
centennial treetops whistling and whining,
too cold to re-experience.

We tumble in small pieces to the ruin next door
now aloft, steady in the wind.
The ghosts suffuse the walls, puff out their chests,
shake their shoulders,
benevolent and confused.
Is this still home?

4 Weather report of the mind

The lines are dropped, baited with breath.
Today's prediction: scattered squalls of doubt.

5 Primeval soup

That first creature must have crawled out of the sea
on a day like this.

The sky as indeterminate air, hovering nearly liquid,
a cosy escape for a budding amphibian.

6 Drifting northward

No whitecaps on this sea.
Just this soft grey, fluid purple,
like the sunlight of Aswan.

Branches jut out like petrified sea monsters,
beaks and snouts ready to snag a ship,
drag it down and under.

Ochre, sienna, blue-black, moss green,
a lake in the sky
reflects chunks of onyx below.

7 Ready for launch

Curled up to the edge
of my skin.
Destined to meet yours
in a drumbeat.

Dropped into a pot,
a posse, of you and me.

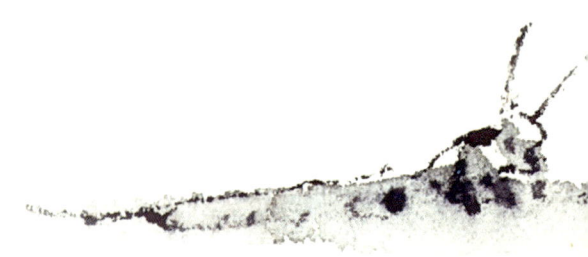

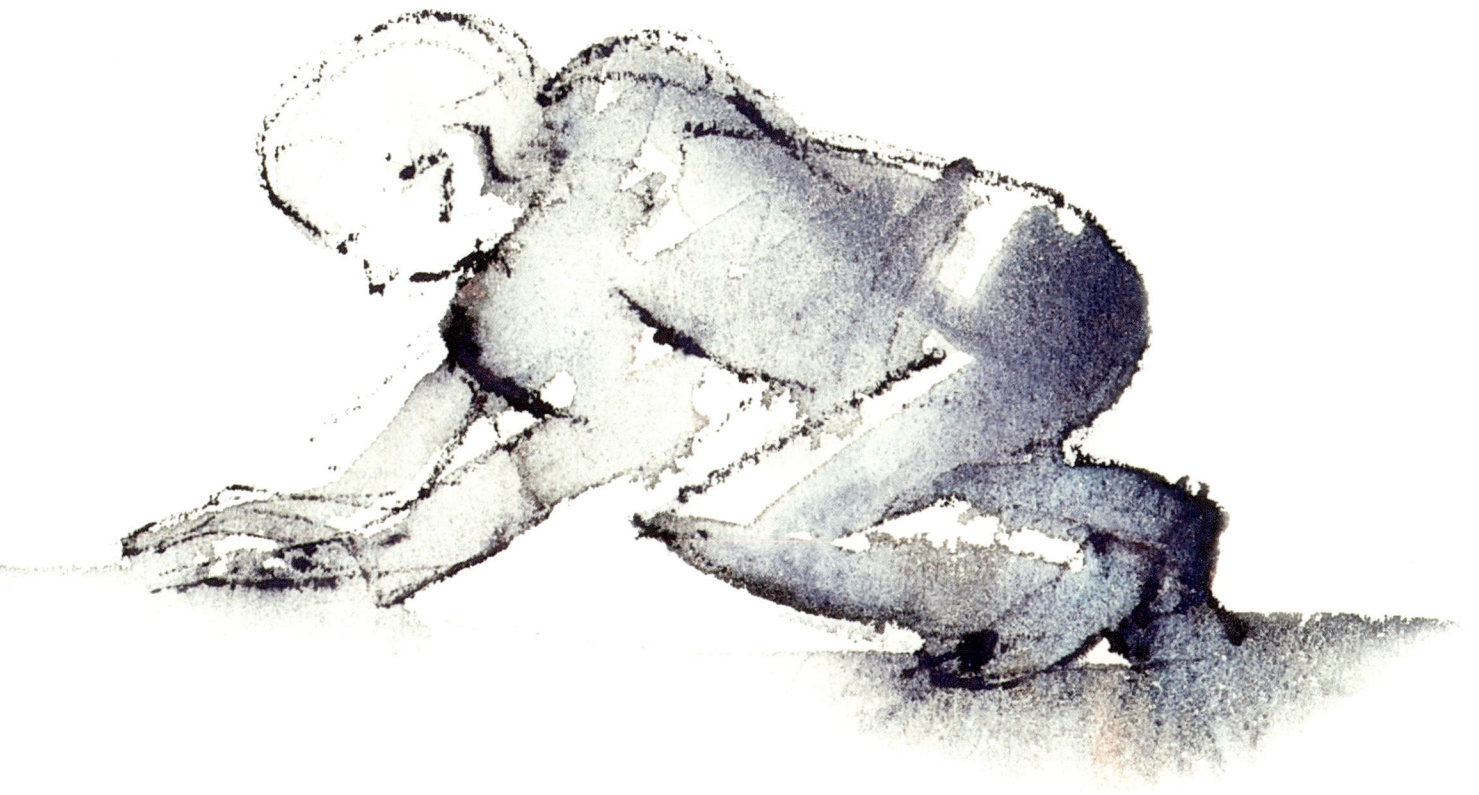

8 Ode to the scapegoat

When lightning strikes, as it does,
pause a moment,
and consider yourself lucky.
Behind, trails of dusty disappointment;
ahead, a full deck of promise.

9 In the jar

You keep a butterfly in a jar,
always one just in case:
each one beautiful,
perfect in limb and wing;
flight contained,
so much promise,
so much grace.

Stop at now,
a perfect moment;
no then, no when,
no future.

The shadows on the wall
collapse in shards to the floor.

10

Saddling up

A good cowboy needs a quick and
nimble mount;
before climbing in the saddle,
it's always a good idea
to check the hindquarters.

II Gossips

Like a winged thief,
stealing a tidbit,
a slice of information,
a juicy bit,
only to drop it on another plate,
preening with the pride of reflected knowledge;
bubbles captured, never ingested,
never digested –
plucked from one host,
infecting another.

12 Snake oil

A pseudo-magician with sticky paws
quenches the burn
— or so he says —
with a slinky swipe.

Another miracle confirmed.

13 Second sight

Striding, arms out – listening, for what?
underground sonar? picking up scents?

Tumbling down, tumbling up, in slow motion,
teetering just far enough off the beat,
but not enough to flounder.

You, confident, in the darkest night.
Blind sight, your gift.
Directions fail you.
Mist helps, moonless nights, too.

These are not metaphors.
Your compass needle floats,
not on mercury, but on fog and figments.

14 Caught or not

Treading water under the dock, a murky night, a game of tag,
it's all so black and spooky.
Water laps and slaps, tugging the pilings, pulling us under.
We float barely, still and breathless,
up to our ears, years of experience, slipping below the surface, silenced.
We are, as always, untouched.
We're too wily, too slippery for that midnight ruse.

15 Flight plan

There was this guy I knew, he lived with a monkey and a tiger. He raced cars, spent a night inside a pyramid and kept searching for Atlantis until he died. A con man who swindled or enlightened, depending. He read auras: at a dinner table, the ballerina gleamed gold; the matriarch, emerald — and me? Nothing shimmers around me, apparently, and I peddle a pack of lies.

But I did learn this:
when passing a car on a race course, keep all rivals in your peripheral vision — and focus, fix, will yourself, ten seconds, three metres into the future. Leave them in the dust. It's a flawless flight plan.

16 It's a dull mind that only believes what it sees

It's a dull mind that only believes what it sees.

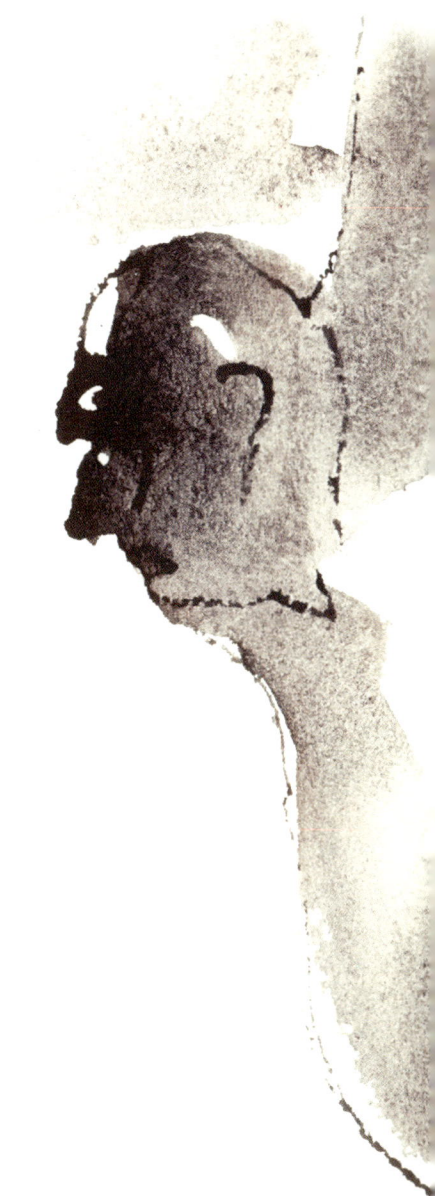

17 Watching time pass

Layering past to future:
   it's the transformation,
      the point where the inanimate
         leans hard enough forward
           to push time to the brink.

           Or maybe more like hurtling
             into a field theory of mind.

18 No re-entry

It's chaos down there,
best to stay in flight;
let the earth revolve underneath us, and
remain aloft for another day or week or so.

Down below, the land is spattered with burst balloons,
odd creatures are abroad.
Cats claw at the windows, frantic for entry;
that darkness has teeth.

19 Impenetrable solution

The snake that curls lifeless for a week,
sated, digesting its latest prey,
is awake again, hungry again.
Coiled, competing, calling.

And how to tear away
from that siren on the rocks,
that beckoning beauty.
Either way spells defeat.

You, already in stop action
before stepping off the edge.
You, manoeuvring through the station,
a picture every three seconds.

A picture every three seconds.
  Three beats of the heart
    for each beat on the screen,
      and only a handful left.

        Maybe you veered to the east
          in the blanks in-between;
            lured by empty,
              safe in black.

20 *Life on the farm*

Why did that lizard jump into the pot?
There are birds in the kitchen,
spiders in the sink as big as the drain,
geckos skittering across the floor,
cats fighting in the attic,
a wild boar laid out on the table outside,
a cuckoo mocking from the treetops,
kestrels bringing up their brood,
toads croaking in the pond,
crows beating against the bedroom window,
birds swooping through the rafters,
wisteria tendrils winding through a closed window,
bees in the roof beams, and honey, yes honey, dripping down the walls.
Swarming; it's possible, just possible, that we are superfluous here.

21 Breathing underwater

A cluster of flight,
which direction home?
There was that dream last night
about an electric fireball dead ahead,
taking your hands off the wheel
to soar straight into uncertainty.
What a relief.

22 Maelstrom

The owl, invincible,
sailed safe from the storm raging on,
like the wind howling down the Rhône,
blowing blisters on trees with
a fever that wouldn't break.

23 Bury her deep

Dump her into a stagnant pool
next to sacks of garbage,
a torn Carrefour bag,
empty tuna cans,
wadded-up toilet paper,
an encrusted razor, disposable,
a pyramid,
empty wine bottles, three cracked.
And bury her deep.

24 Entrapped

One page is not enough, not two.
Falling into those eyes would be a bad choice.
Looking out with your view,
hulking, dark souls circling your heart
like beads on a pin cushion –
lovers hurting, the prick, others still aspiring.

All but one, blanketed white, not yet captured.
All that embroidery,
have you any idea how many you
have trapped with that heart?

Every single one believing it was theirs alone.
It must make for a heavy heart,
but that's only a guess.
How to sustain all that,
maybe there never was a choice.

25 Unfettered

I saw you standing on the table the other night,
cast from resin,
chiselled from plaster.
Leaning on your crutches, all grey in suit and tie.
Silent, listening,
the crux in the crutch,
weighted to the future.

I'd take you home, steal you off that perch,
steady you on my table,
grey suit and tie, crutches.
Voodoo you, magic me,
you as large as the hole you left behind.

So startled to see you standing on that table.
I thought you'd have lost those crutches by now.

26 Odd child out

The black sheep was born
on a dark day, inside and out.
She dropped to a muddy slope,
below the blackberry bushes,
and trembled her way to her feet,
a shadow of a promise.

27 Dancer indifferent

The beat drops,
you exit the dance
a beckoning beauty, bare.

Behind, drums hammer on,
unbidden, down low.
Their focus keen, and happy dumb.

Blinkered and united,
a single direction,
following Hamelin's piper home.

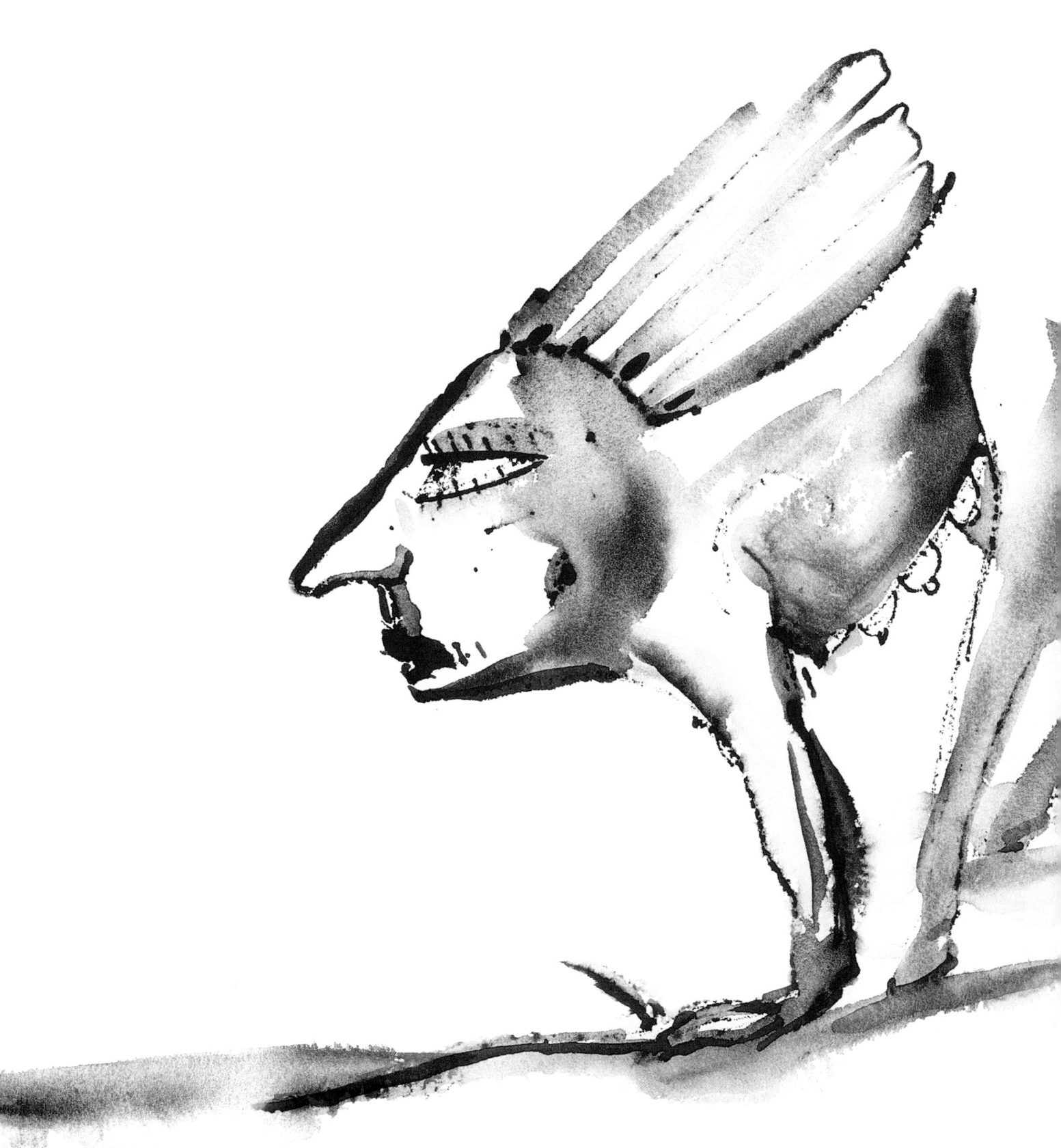

28 Devil's punchbowl

You see a cube of glass,
glistening with grey dust, the
solidified smoke of yesterday's spat.

I see an engineered bird's wing of
transparency, edges sharp enough to shred
the air we breathe.

The battle for silence, finely focused,
perched on a razor's edge.

You ask, when, still, tomorrow?
I say now; it's crystal clear.

29 Sister ships

These ships, lashed together for so long,
cargo shifted back and forth so often,
who knows anymore who's at the wheel,
which engine runs,
whose sail is torn,
which hull leaks,
which one needs caulking.

30 *Such a night*

Raindrops dancing on a still lake,
kicking up sparks of splattering water,
ebbing into mingled twilight.

31 Scaling time

We're skittering around under branch, bud and leaf.
Careening, in alternate time
as blurred bugs.

Roots, blind to what goes on above.
Crusty aged chestnuts keep watch, stalling centuries,
with no ambition to leave a trace.

On this scale of significance,
we are as twigs.

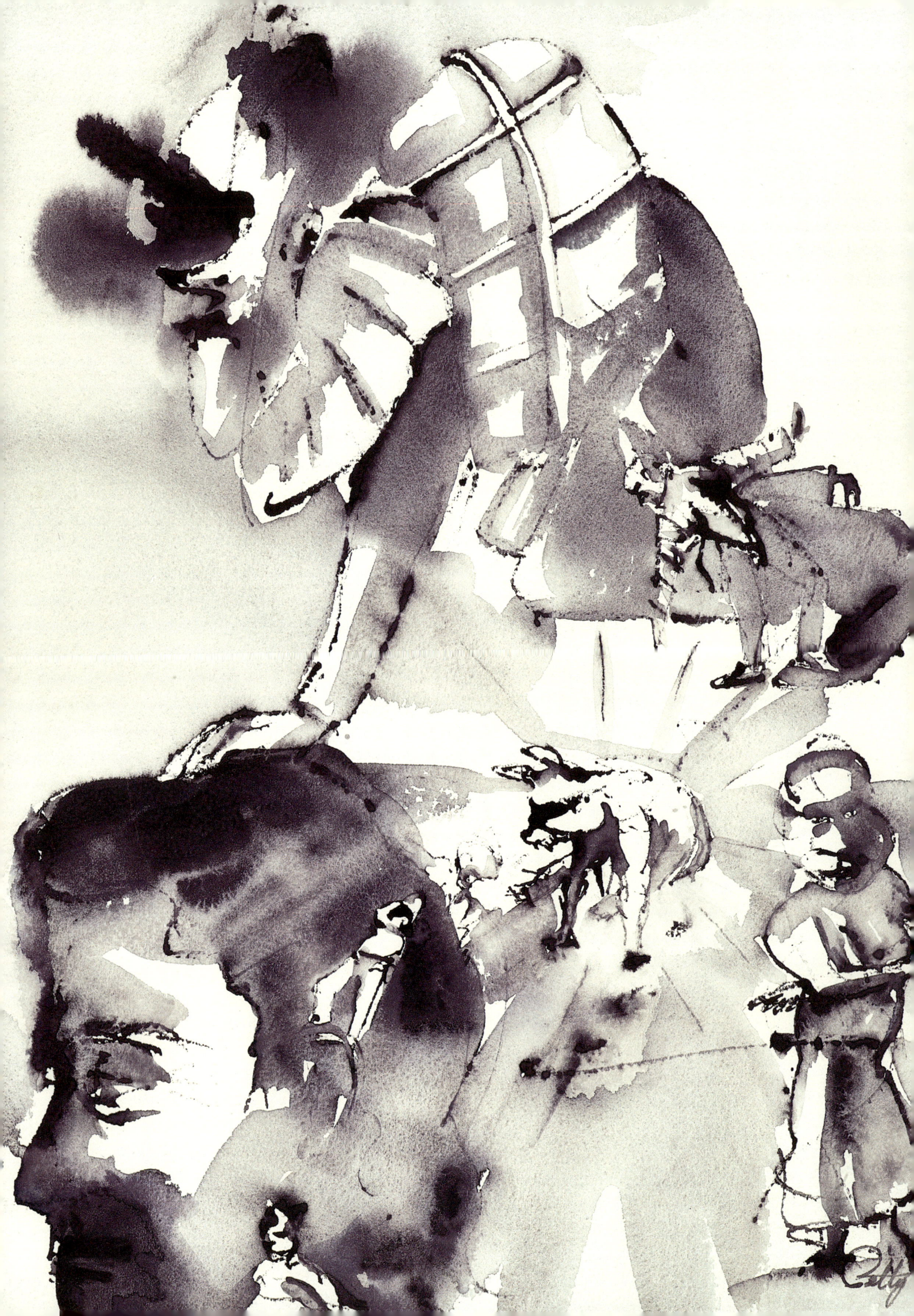

32 Life goes on

Under crumbling chestnut leaves
bulges a cèpe;
a snail speeds over to devour.

A haunch of wild boar
on the front step,
the bullet still buried deep.

The cuckoo lands high in a tree,
steals a nest.
Down tumbles a baby bird.

Bees swarm over the terrace,
a queen unmoored.
Five thousand wings roar in the sky.

COLOPHON

We would like to thank NUM STIBBE, ORNAN ROTEM and MONA GAINER-SALIM of Sylph Editions for their adventurous spirits and artistic talents in the collaborative creation of *Breathing Underwater*, along with Elizabeth Ayre for her eagle eye, as always.

All images: ©RALPH PETTY, 2016
Poems: ©LISA DAVIDSON, 2016

The book is set in Requiem, printed and bound in the UK by Zone Graphics on Olin Natural.

Designed by Ornan Rotem

ISBN: 978-1-90963115-1

SYLPH EDITIONS · LONDON · 2016

www.sylpheditions.com